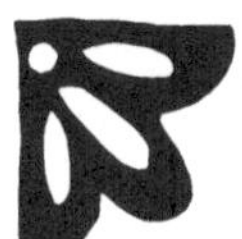

TH 7 STEPS TO ELEGANT Cursive Handwriting

MASTER THE ART OF BEAUTIFUL PENMANSHIP

RICCA'S GARDEN

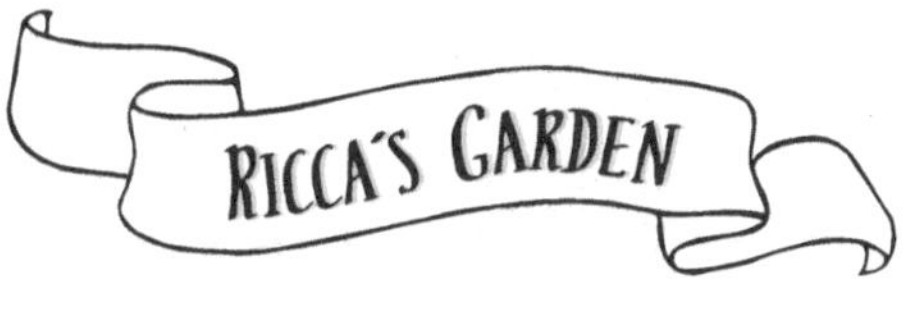

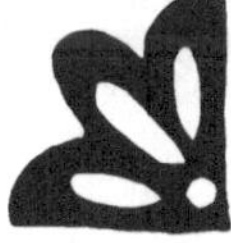

Interested in Hand Lettering?

ricca_garden

info@riccagarden.com

Published & Designed in Brisbane, Australia

First print: Sep 2023

Table of Contents

INTRODUCTION

Welcome to, 'The 7 Steps to Elegant Cursive Handwriting!' Whether you are looking to develop your cursive writing skills, refine your technique and style, or simply embark on a creative and relaxing hobby, I'm sure you will find this book has it all.

In **Step 1**, we'll cover the basics, including posture and pen grip, setting a strong foundation for your cursive writing journey. **Step 2** focuses on mastering basic strokes, providing essential building blocks for forming beautiful letters. Moving forward, **Step 3** guides you through lowercase letters, while **Step 4** introduces uppercase letters, further expanding your skills.

Step 5 is dedicated to the art of joining letters seamlessly, creating a fluid and elegant flow in your writing. In **Step 6**, you'll have the opportunity to showcase all your acquired skills by working on graceful flourishes to add a touch of personality.

Finally, in **Step 7**, we'll demonstrate how to write numbers beautifully, rounding off your journey to mastering elegant cursive handwriting.

Each step builds upon the previous one, providing a comprehensive and structured approach to help you achieve the elegance you desire in your cursive writing.

While you probably know that developing your handwriting skills will be an enjoyable activity, there are a few things you may not know. Writing by hand has surprising benefits—it's calming and has been shown to slow the heartbeat, bringing us back into the moment, thus relieving stress.

Moreover, another powerful writing practice called freewriting can have a profound impact on our minds. Freewriting involves writing our thoughts freely by hand, without directing our writing but simply letting our thoughts flow onto the page. Not only does freewriting improve the neural connection in our brains, but it also sparks creativity that can flow into other areas of our lives.

Through freewriting, we can explore emotions that may be buried deep inside, bringing them to the surface. Additionally, it can greatly help us process thoughts and feelings that may be twisted and tangled, and need to be unraveled.

There are numerous benefits to handwriting that go beyond the simple enjoyment of practicing and honing your skills. Handwriting helps strengthen our fine motor skills, which have sadly been neglected in this digital age of quick emails and shortened text messages.

As you progress in your cursive writing journey, you'll discover various writing styles you might admire and aspire to develop. However, it's essential to remember that each of us possesses a unique writing style, and that uniqueness is something to celebrate! Once you can identify the signs of your own style, allow it to flow naturally—that's your distinct style, and it's wonderful!

Our handwriting, unlike typing an email, often reflects our personalities in fascinating ways. A rushed writing style may indicate a person who leads a busy life or tends to do things in a hurry. On the other hand, a very neat writing style may reflect someone who values organization and neatness in various aspects of their lives.

Have you ever wondered what your writing reveals about you? It can be fascinating to explore it!

In this book, we cover everything you need to know, from handwriting terminology and essential tools of the trade to extensive cursive writing practice—of course! We'll share tips to help you maintain consistent shape and slant in your writing while also adding delightful flourishes.

Lastly, for all the lefties out there, you'll be fine! We've got you covered with some tips to follow.

LET'S GET INTO IT!

Step 1: Let's Talk Basics!

I know—you just want to dive in and get started! But first things first because who wants to go through trial and error when you can get the professional heads up before you start? We'll talk basics briefly, such as terminology, pen grip and posture, tools, and consistency, then you're good to go.

Let's get started!

Terminology

There are a few basic words to learn that will come up from time to time throughout this book. Let's go through them:

2nd ascender
1st ascender
meanline
baseline
1st descender
2nd descender
Handwriting
Crossbar
Flourish
X-Height
Counter
Descending Loop

Baseline The baseline is your base, and keeps your letters from going off track—which is easy to do if you forget your baseline.

X-Height This is the distance between the baseline and the meanline (the height of the lowercase x)

1st & 2nd Ascender Lines These are the lines where the tips of taller letters meet.

1st & 2nd Descender Lines These are the lines which guide you in writing letters that dip below the baseline.

Meanline Remember 'M' for middle—this is your middle line, the imaginary spot where the tops of most of your lowercase letters will be. Keep in mind there are also letters like l, k, and b that do reach the ascender line.

Counter This is the negative space in a letter—the empty enclosed space such as the spaces you find in a, p, and d.

Crossbars Crossbars are those horizontal lines across letters such as in the letter t.

Flourishes Flourishes are a great way to show your personality, have a bit of fun and add some style to your letters.

Tools

You will probably have a lot of the tools already, but you may wish to add a particular pen type or color you'd like to try out. It's best to start off with what you have until you get the hang of things, and then you can always add more.

Pencils: Great for practicing and getting used to the letterform.

Eraser: Your best friend when practicing!

Pens: You can begin by practicing with any pen you have lying around, or by experimenting with various pen tips and colors. For a more personalized experience, you may even consider exploring the world of fountain pens. With fountain pens, you have the freedom to experiment with different nib sizes and ink options. Feel free to add flair and personality to your writing with shimmering inks or chrome shading inks!

Paper: Do yourself a favor and use paper with guidelines to begin with. You might like to try using tracing paper if you prefer not to write in this book—but there's always the option of printing out the practice sheets, too.

Position and Posture

You probably already know that slouching or hunching will leave you with a sore neck, shoulders, or back.

So aim to:

- Sit up straight at a desk
- Keep those shoulders relaxed
- Have your feet firmly on the ground

Make sure you check your posture from time to time because it can be easy to be so engrossed in writing that you forget about posture.

Paper Position:

When you tilt the page, it is easier to achieve the slant you want. Keep it tilted to the right if you are left-handed and to the left if you are right-handed.

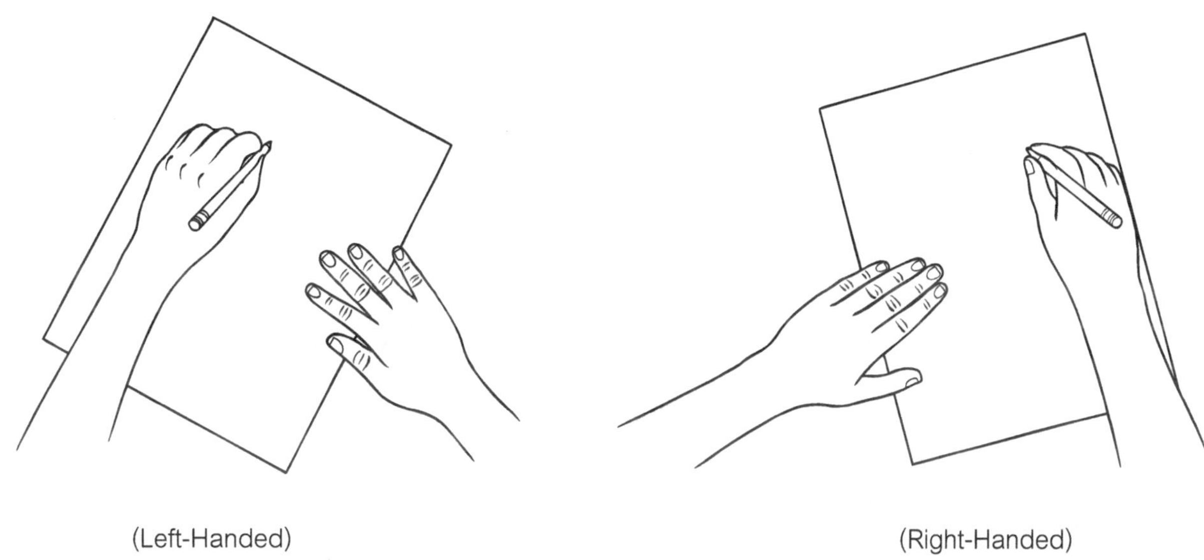

(Left-Handed) (Right-Handed)

Pen Grasp:

Use the tripod grasp, where you hold the pen with 3 fingers: the thumb, middle finger, and index finger. Place your fingers up and away from the tip. The middle finger rests under the pen, while the thumb and index finger gently hold the pen. This is the style usually taught in schools because it allows for good control and prevents cramps or tired hands.

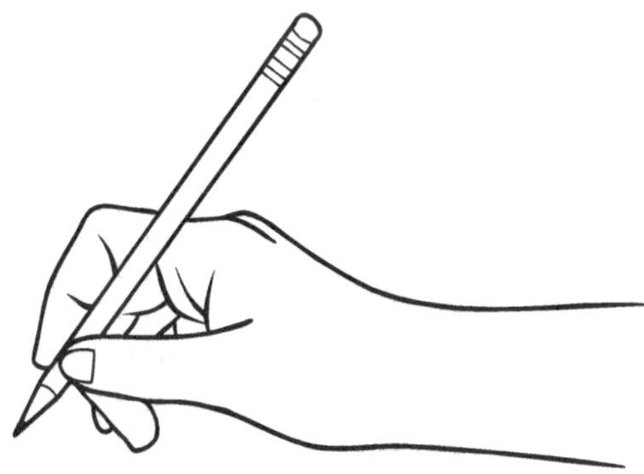

Remember not to grip your pen too tightly. No white knuckles (you'll get too tired!) Relax—there's no hurry and the pen won't fall out of your grip easily.

Tips for left-handed lovelies:

Take some extra time to experiment with your pen grip until you find what feels most comfortable for you. Some people prefer to place their hand underneath the baseline to avoid smudging the ink, while others may find positioning their hand above the baseline more comfortable. Remember, there are no strict rules, so do what feels right for you. Nevertheless, aim to grip the pen 2–3 cm away from the tip for better visibility while writing. Opting for a pen with fast-drying ink can help prevent smudging too.

Feel free to rotate the paper as needed to find the most comfortable angle for your writing. Above all, savor the process and take your time. Writing should be a relaxing, creative, and enjoyable experience!

Care about consistency!

Consistency is crucial when it comes to handwriting as it can greatly impact the overall appearance. Here are some handy tips to help you maintain consistency in key areas:

Slant: Maintaining a consistent slant in your writing is essential for a pleasing appearance. To achieve this, you can draw a little line under each letter to indicate its angle and see if the letters are matching up nicely.

Spacing: Always stop to check your work to make sure you have even spacing between the letters and words. The exact amount of spacing can vary based on personal preference and writing styles. The essential principle remains: strive for consistency.

Shape/Style: Take a moment to think about your preferred writing style. Do you lean towards a more rounded or angular appearance? Whichever way you prefer, strive to keep the style consistent within a piece of work.

Size: Are you keeping your letters consistent in size? This is when guidelines are handy. Make sure you follow them diligently, so your letters remain uniform throughout your writing.

Document your journey!

In the future, it might be rewarding to see just how much you've improved since you began your cursive writing journey! Try writing this inspiring phrase below:

"Writing is the painting of the voice." - Voltaire

Don't forget to date it! ___/___/___

___/___/___

___/___/___

___/___/___

___/___/___

___/___/___

DON'T FORGET TO CHECK BACK IN TO SEE HOW MUCH YOU'VE PROGRESSED.

Step 2:
Basic Strokes Practice

In Step 2, we will focus on mastering basic strokes, emphasizing consistency through regular practice.

BASIC STOKES

Improving consistency in your cursive writing is a primary goal at this stage. By dedicating time to practicing the basic strokes, you will gradually enhance the overall consistency of your writing. It's crucial to be mindful of any potential bad habits that may arise during practice. Nipping them in the bud early on is essential, as correcting them later can prove to be more challenging. Check in with yourself from time to time to make sure you're on track and practicing correctly. Think about your posture, page position, pen grip and spacing.

1. SLANTED STRAIGHT LINE:

Focus on keeping the lines parallel.

2nd A
1st A
M
B
1st D
2nd D

2. UNDER CURVE:

This slant is steeper, and often acts as an entry stroke. Is your slant consistent? Don't worry if it isn't—good practice makes perfect!

2nd A
1st A
M
B
1st D
2nd D

3. OVER CURVE:

Opposite to the Under Curve.

4. UNDERTURN: Is found in letters like i, u, and w.

2nd A
1st A
M
B
1st D
2nd D

5. OVERTURN: Make sure you are starting from the baseline and hitting the meanline before turning. This is found in letters like m and n.

2nd A
1st A
M
B
1st D
2nd D

6. COMPOUND CURVE: Again, take a moment to check the consistency. Are the curves parallel? These are found in letters like h, m, n, v, and x.

2nd A
1st A
M
B
1st D
2nd D

7. LOOP: Work on forming even-shaped loops, taking care to keep them similar. They are found in letters like b, h, k, l, and f.

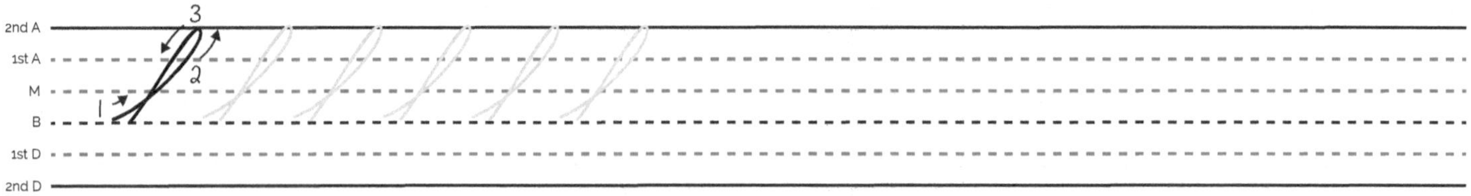

2nd A
1st A
M
B
1st D
2nd D

8. OVAL: Make sure the oval is closed at the top. These are found in letters like a, d, g, o, and q.

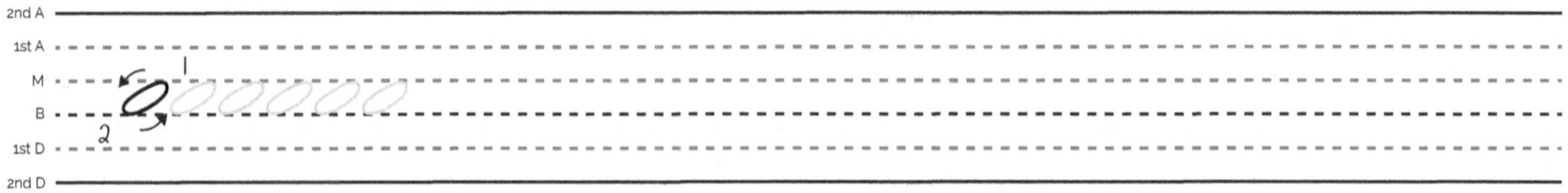

2nd A
1st A
M
B
1st D
2nd D

EXTRA PRACTICE:

Step 3: Lowercase

Let's get into lowercase letters and practice one letter at a time until we feel confident to move on. We want to get this right from the beginning so take your time at this stage.

During our practice, we will be focusing on letters grouped by their shape, rather than following the alphabetical order. This approach is helpful as it allows us to work on letters with similar features together, strengthening our muscle memory.

a b c d e f g

h i j k l m n

o p q r s t u

v w x y z

THINGS TO LOOK OUT FOR WHILE YOU ARE PRACTICING:

- Are you hitting the baseline?
- Is the slant angle parallel? (You can draw the parallel lines to check).

Grab another pen and mark on the page the areas you would like to improve. Of course, there might be lots of areas to improve on at this point so don't be hard on yourself.

Group 1: I, U, W – Working on Underturns

2nd A
1st A
M
B
1st D
2nd D

1 Start by drawing an under curve entry stroke.

2 3 Bring the pen down in order to draw an underturn.

4 Finish up with a dot.

2nd A
1st A
M
B
1st D
2nd D

1 Repeat what you did for i but without a dot.

2 3

4 5 Next, connect it with a second underturn.

2nd A
1st A
M
B
1st D
2nd D

1

2 3 This one is formed similar to u, except the underturn will be narrower.

4 5

6 Finish it with a horizontal curve that will be used to connect to the next letter.

Lowercase

Group 2: n, m, x, v – features overturns and compound curves

2nd A
1st A
M
B
1st D
2nd D

Make an overturn followed by a compound curve.

1 2 3 4

Things to check for here are making sure the stroke is on a consistent slant, and that the spacing is equal.

2nd A
1st A
M
B
1st D
2nd D

The m is the same as n but with 2 overturns.

1 2 3 4 5 6

Take your time and practice getting similar turns and slopes.

2nd A
1st A
M
B
1st D
2nd D

Your x is a compound curve with a slant straight line (the cross going upward).

1 2 3

2nd A
1st A
M
B
1st D
2nd D

Start by drawing a compound curve but just as it turns back up, the turn will be much steeper this time.

Finish it off with a horizontal line for the connecting stroke as you did with w.

GROUP 3: O, A, C, E - FEATURES OVALS/VARIATION OF OVALS (FOR LETTERS C AND E)

2nd A
1st A
M
B
1st D
2nd D

Use a different entry stroke - the over curve.

Avoid leaving the oval open at the top.

Finish up with a nice horizontal connecting stroke.

Lowercase

2nd A
1st A
M
B
1st D
2nd D

Your a will again begin with an over curve.

1 2 3 4 5

Follow by an oval, then an underturn to finish the letter.

2nd A
1st A
M
B
1st D
2nd D

Begin with an entry stroke and make a hook when you reach the meanline.

1 2

Finish with a tight turn at the bottom.

2nd A
1st A
M
B
1st D
2nd D

1 2 3

With your e, make sure to leave enough space for the counter (enclosed white space), so that it is not mistaken for an i, especially when you are using a thicker nib pen.

GROUP 4: L, H, K, B - FEATURES ASCENDING LOOP

Lowercase

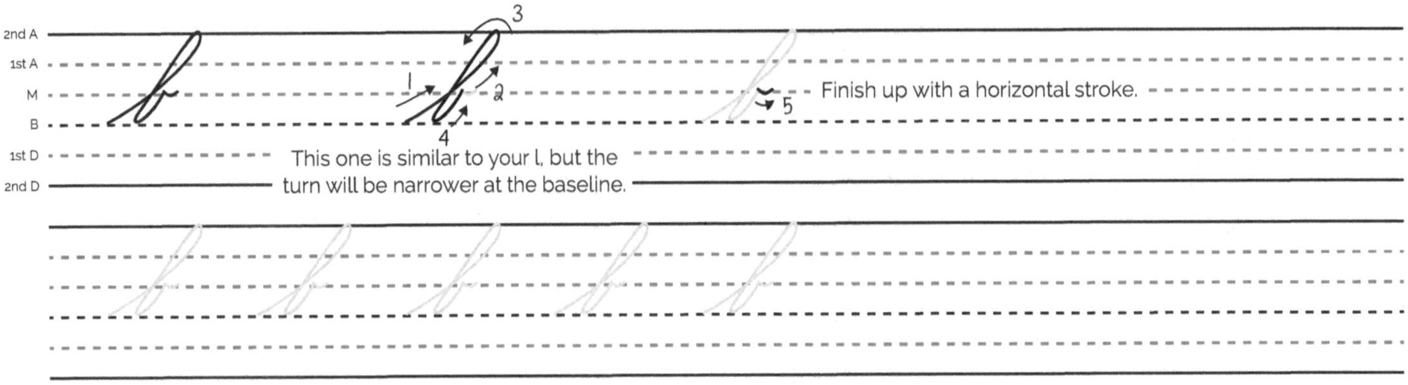

2nd A
1st A
M
B
1st D
2nd D
1
2
3
4
5
This one is similar to your l, but the turn will be narrower at the baseline.
Finish up with a horizontal stroke.

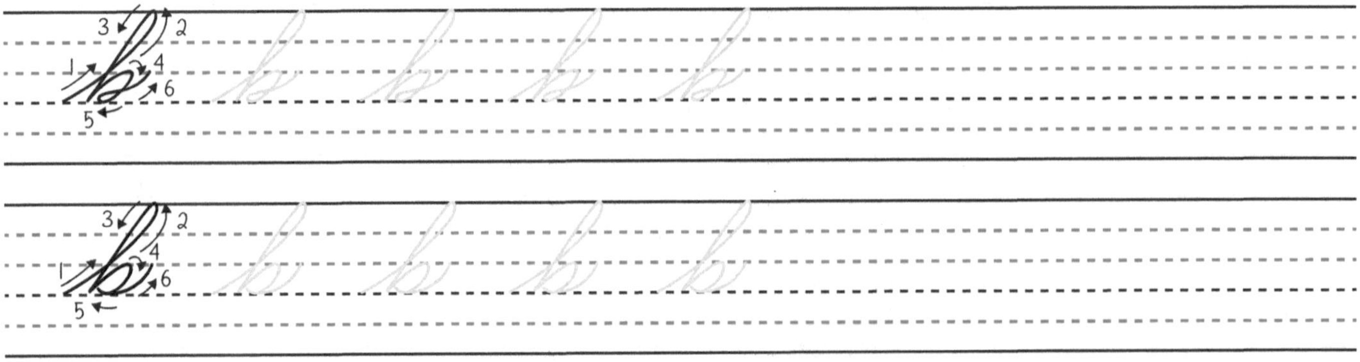

1
2
3
4
5
6

Group 5: J, Y, G, Z – Features Descending Loop

2nd A
1st A
M
B
1st D
2nd D
1
2
3
Starts with an entry stroke and a descending loop.
4. Add the dot at the end.

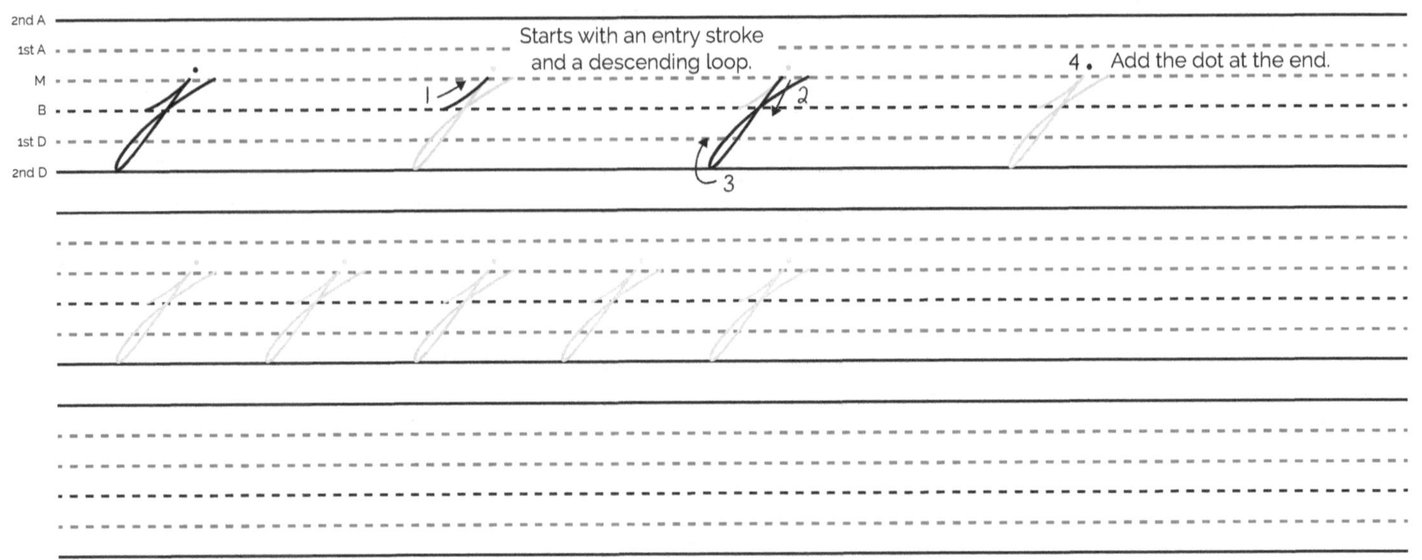

2nd A
1st A
M
B
1st D
2nd D

Begin your y with a compound curve and move on to a descending loop.

1 2 3 4 5

2nd A
1st A
M
B
1st D
2nd D

Begin just as you would when writing an a but instead of an underturn, complete a descending loop.

1 2 3 4 5 6

Are the angles of your loops matching up?

2nd A
1st A
M
B
1st D
2nd D

Write your z with an overturn with a descending loop.

1 2 3 4

GROUP 6: T, D, P – FEATURES SEMI-EXTENDED LETTERS

2nd A
1st A
M
B
1st D
2nd D

Begin with an entry stroke.

Add a crossbar to complete the letter.

From the 1st ascender line, descend on a slant and make a tight turn right on the baseline.

Form the letter d just like the lowercase a at the beginning.

Complete the letter with an extended underturn that starts at the 1st ascender line.

Begin with an entry stroke that extends up to the 1st ascender line.

Descend with a slanted straight line and complete the letter with a compound curve.

2nd A
1st A
M
B
1st D
2nd D

GROUP 7: F, Q - A VARIATION OF DESCENDING LOOP

First, form an ascending loop then a reversed descending loop.

2nd A
1st A
M
B
1st D
2nd D

Finish with a curve line that connects to the next letter.

2nd A
1st A
M
B
1st D
2nd D

Begin writing the letter just as you would for the lowercase letter a.

Sweep the line down and come right back up, keeping the angle level with your downstroke.

Lowercase

Group 8: R, S – Letters that go above the meanline

2nd A
1st A
M
B
1st D
2nd D

Start off with an entry stroke that reaches slightly above the meanline.

1 2 3 4

Descend with a slight curve to the right, followed by a tight underturn.

1 2 3

2nd A
1st A
M
B
1st D
2nd D

Begin your s with an entry stroke that goes up slightly above the meanline.

1 2

Descend with a curve to the left.

3

Come back up again with a curve that extends to the meanline.

1 2 3 4

EXTRA PRACTICE

So how did you get on with your lowercase letters? I'm sure you did really well, and it's completely normal to need a little or a lot of improvement which will simply come from 'good' practice.

Before moving on to the next step, take a moment to look over your writing and see where you feel there's room for improvement. Maybe you need to work on your spacing or slant? Or if your body has any aches or pains, now is a good time to check your posture and make any adjustments before carrying on.

STEP 4: UPPERCASE

Uppercase letters are quite different to lowercase letters as you will soon see. Don't be intimidated though—it's just different, not more difficult!

A B C D E

F G H I J

K L M N O

P Q R S T U

V W X Y Z

Uppercase

Group 1: O, C, E, D - Direct oval capitals

2nd A
1st A
M
B
1st D
2nd D

Next, sweep your pen down to match your first downward stroke.

As you move back up, make a parallel curve.

Start on the ascender line, and make a curve downwards until you hit the baseline.

2nd A
1st A
M
B
1st D
2nd D

Begin your uppercase C with a loop, then draw an open oval shape.

2nd A
1st A
M
B
1st D
2nd D

This letter builds on the skills you just learned for C and O. Begin with a small loop, then come back down and draw the first small oval from the top.

Loop around on the first ascender line to connect the bottom oval.

Your D will begin on the first ascender line. Then move your way down on a slight slant before looping down to the baseline.

2nd A
1st A
M
B
1st D
2nd D

1 2 3 4 5

Draw the oval from the bottom.

GROUP 2: N, M, H, K, U, V, W, X, Q, J, Y, Z – REVERSED OVAL CAPITALS

Let's practice the basic reversed oval shape before moving on to letters.

2nd A
1st A
M
B
1st D
2nd D

1 2

2nd A
1st A
M
B
1st D
2nd D

1 2

Start off with a reversed oval.

3 4

Then, draw a narrow overturn, then a narrow compound curve.

5 6 7

The height should be lowered each time. Keep the same slant!

Uppercase

2nd A
1st A
M
B
1st D
2nd D

1 2 3 4 5

N starts off with a reversed oval from the baseline.

Draw a nice narrow compound curve. The height should be below the reversed oval.

2nd A
1st A
M
B
1st D
2nd D

1 2 3 4

Begin H with a reversed oval, followed by a slanted line.

Finish up with a lovely curved horizontal line.

2nd A
1st A
M
B
1st D
2nd D

1 2 3 4 5

Begin with a reversed oval.

Next, draw a slanted line from the top ascender line, continue with a small loop, and connect to the bottom part.

Finish off the letter with an underturn.

2nd A
1st A
M
B
1st D
2nd D

1 2 3

Begin your uppercase U with a reversed oval. Without stopping at the baseline, continue to come up to the 1st ascender line.

4 5

Finish with an underturn that is slightly longer in the beginning.

2nd A
1st A
M
B
1st D
2nd D

1 2 3

Your V will begin in a very similar way to the first part of U, except the turn is much narrower.

2nd A
1st A
M
B
1st D
2nd D

1 2

The letter W starts off with a reversed oval.

3 4

Come back up with a slanted line, then back down again to the baseline.

5

Up you go again, but only to the 1st ascender line this time.

Uppercase

2nd A
1st A
M
B
1st D
2nd D

1 2

3 4

Finish it off by drawing a half oval shape to form your X.

Begin your X with a reversed oval.

2nd A
1st A
M
B
1st D
2nd D

1 2

Continue to draw a horizontal loop at the baseline.

4

3

Begin with a reversed oval.

Are the shapes of your letters matching up?

2nd A
1st A
M
B
1st D
2nd D

2

1

This time the reversed oval is a lot narrower. Draw a nice descending loop when you pass the baseline.

5

4

3

Your Y will be similar to the capital U.

2nd A
1st A
M
B
1st D
2nd D

1 2 3 4 5 6 7

Finish off with a descending loop.

Begin Z with a reversed oval.

2nd A
1st A
M
B
1st D
2nd D

1 2 3 4 5 6

Draw a small loop at the baseline and finish with a descending loop.

Group 3: T, F, L, A, I, S, G - Capital Stem Letters

We are moving to the next group of letters with capital stem. Let's start off again by practicing the basic shape.

2nd A
1st A
M
B
1st D
2nd D

1 2 3

Uppercase

2nd A
1st A
M
B
1st D
2nd D
3
1
2
4
5
Draw a horizontal line with a small loop at the beginning.
Begin a little below the 2nd ascender line, then draw the capital stem.
4
1
3
2
5
6
7
Finish off with a small slanted line.
Draw a horizontal line with a small loop at the beginning.
Start slightly below the 2nd ascender line, then draw the capital stem. Continue to cross the stem.
Start your uppercase L with a small loop, leading into a capital stem.
Extend into another small horizontal loop along the baseline. Finish by curving up slightly.

2nd A
1st A
M
B
1st D
2nd D

Draw another slanted line between the 2nd ascender line and the baseline.

Draw a curved horizontal line.

Draw a capital stem for your A.

2nd A
1st A
M
B
1st D
2nd D

Begin by drawing a curved line from the baseline to the 2nd ascender line, and remember the slant as you go down. Do an oval turn and connect to a capital stem.

2nd A
1st A
M
B
1st D
2nd D

Once you reach the ascender line, draw a loop and connect up to the capital stem.

Begin S on the baseline and draw a slanted line from the left.

UPPERCASE

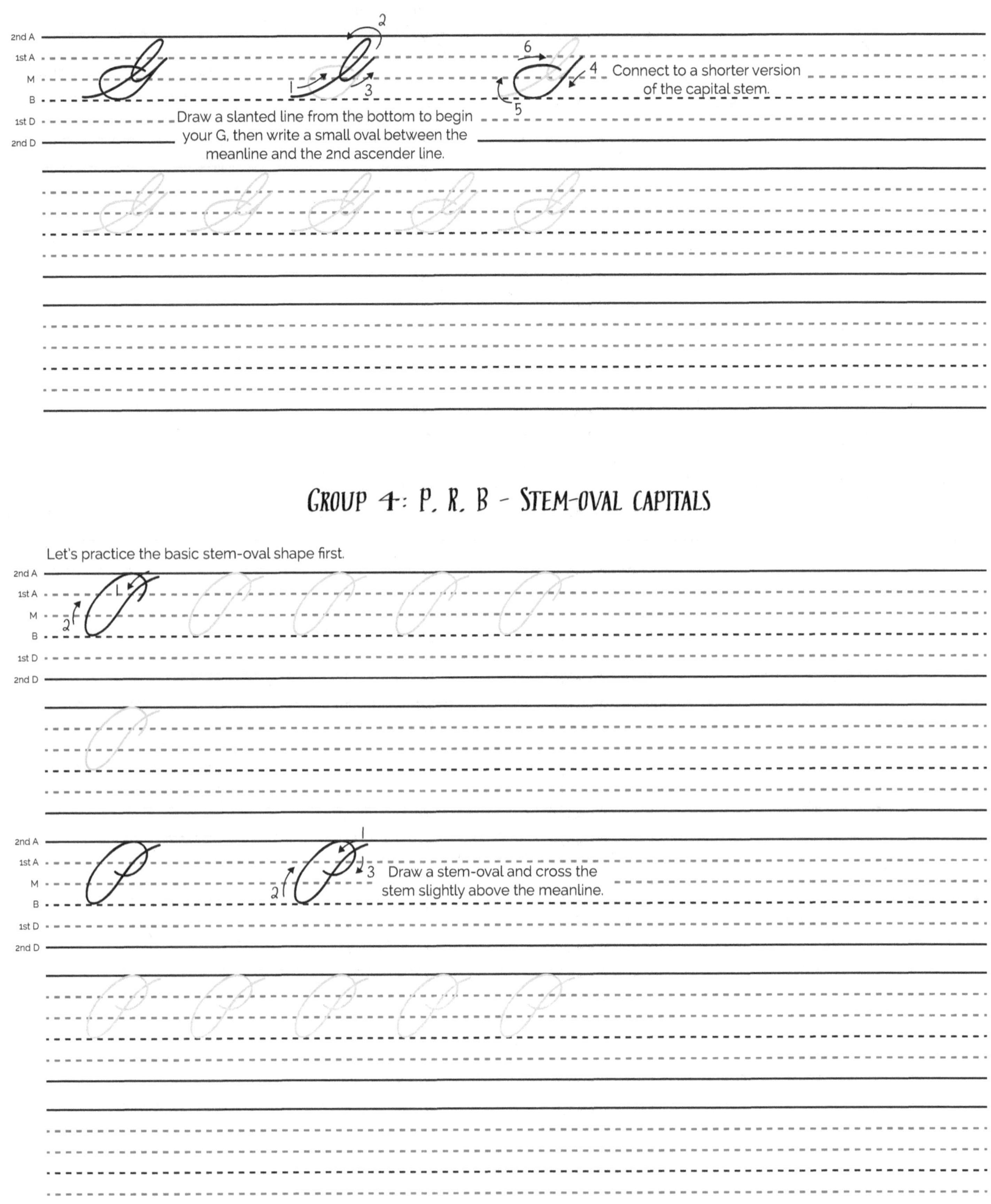

GROUP 4: P, R, B - STEM-OVAL CAPITALS

2nd A
1st A
M
B
1st D
2nd D

Draw a stem-oval and do a small loop slightly above the meanline.

Connect the bottom underturn.

2nd A
1st A
M
B
1st D
2nd D

Start by drawing a stem-oval, followed by a small loop slightly above the meanline. Connect the partial oval.

Uppercase Variations

Okay, I'm sure you're getting the hang of it now! Let's try another variation to mix things up and build on your growing skills!

2nd A
1st A
M
B
1st D
2nd D

1 2 3

2nd A
1st A
M
B
1st D
2nd D

1 2 3 4 5 6

2nd A
1st A
M
B
1st D
2nd D

1 2 3 4

2nd A
1st A
M
B
1st D
2nd D
1
2
3
4
5
2nd A
1st A
M
B
1st D
2nd D
1
2
3
4
5
2nd A
1st A
M
B
1st D
2nd D
1
2
3
4
5
6

Uppercase Variations

2nd A
1st A
M
B
1st D
2nd D
1
2
3
4
5
6

Uppercase Variations

2nd A
1st A
M
B
1st D
2nd D
1
4
5
2
3
2nd A
1st A
M
B
1st D
2nd D
2
1
3
5
4
2nd A
1st A
M
B
1st D
2nd D
1
4
3
2
5

Uppercase Variations

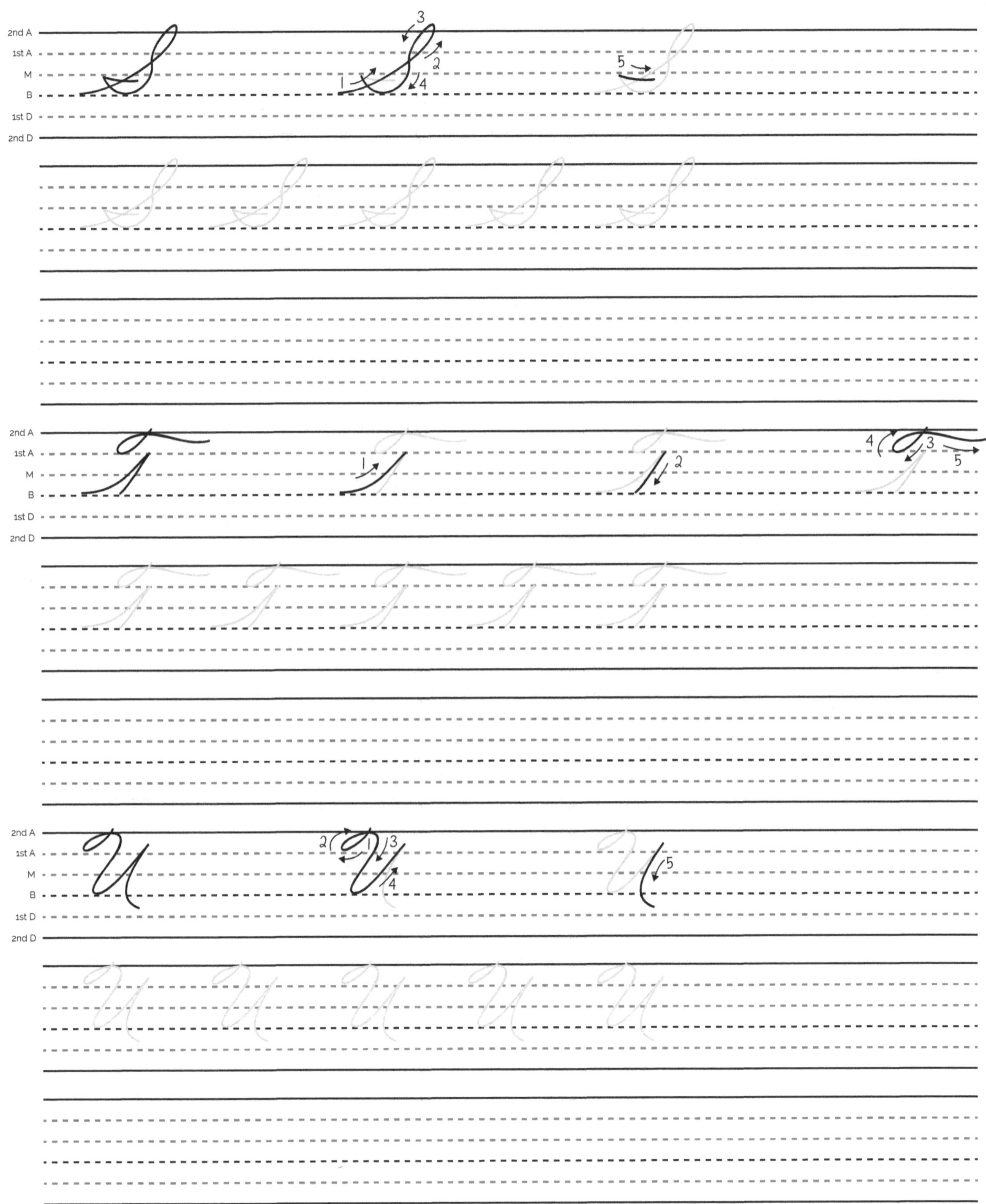

2nd A
1st A
M
B
1st D
2nd D
2
1
3
4
2nd A
1st A
M
B
1st D
2nd D
2
1
3
4
5
6
2nd A
1st A
M
B
1st D
2nd D
2
1
3
4
5

Uppercase Variations

2nd A
1st A
M
B
1st D
2nd D

2nd A
1st A
M
B
1st D
2nd D

2nd A
1st A
M
B
1st D
2nd D

Step 5: Joining Letters

You've reached an exciting part of your writing journey - joining up those letters you've been practicing so much! Don't worry if you're a little wobbly or inconsistent at first—you'll get there with practice. Just keep on checking that you're consistent and follow the tips below. Enjoy!

Tips on connecting your letters

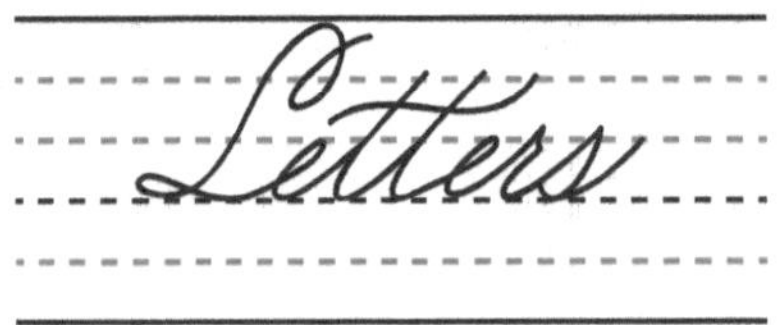

Consistency is Key:

The way you connect letters should always be consistent throughout—maintain a consistent slant, consistent spacing, and consistent letter size and shape. Did I mention consistency?

Take Your Time:

Always take your time, and make sure the letter formation is done properly before continuing.

Master Tricky Connections:

There are many letters that simply flow naturally into each other—we like that! But that's not always the case. Some letters have an exit stroke that begins on the meanline (e.g., b, o, v, w). In these cases, the connection point might not be clear and might therefore take some practice to get right and to get used to how these letters will flow on. For example, when connecting o and s, you can drop the exit stroke slightly to make a better connection.

Look Ahead:

Know what letter you are writing next—always look ahead! This will be easier with practice but do try to look ahead and your pen will naturally follow as you are prepared for the next letter.

Take the word 'change' as an example:

1. When you are connecting to a letter that has an ascender or descender, you'll notice a longer movement in your writing. Take a moment to slow down and ensure that the ascender reaches its upper guideline, and the descender reaches its lower guidelines.

2. When connecting a, g, or other oval-shape letters) you will need to stretch the connecting stroke slightly longer.

Stay Relaxed:

Always maintaining a relaxed grip will greatly assist with smooth connections and fluid writing.

Capital Letter Connections:

You don't need to connect all capital letters to lowercase ones. Some capital letters that are hard to connect are F, P, V, and W. It is completely up to you whether you would like to connect them or not.

Personalize Your Practice:

When practicing, why not create a word list based on themes you love, or try writing some quotes/poems/song lyrics that inspire you? As always, remember—consistency!

Joining Letters

First let's practice Group 1 letters that feature the underturn.

2nd A
1st A
M
B
1st D
2nd D

iu *iu* *iu*

uu *uu* *uu*

ui *ui* *ui*

Now have a go at Group 2 letters that feature overturns and compound curves.

2nd A
1st A
M
B
1st D
2nd D

mn *mn* *mn*

mv *mv* *mv*

nu *nu* *nu*

ai *ai* *ai*

min *min* *min*

Notice here how we connect i and n—make use of a reversed compound curve:

GROUP 3 LETTERS FEATURE OVALS AND VARIATIONS OF OVALS (LETTERS C AND E).

2nd A
1st A
M
B
1st D
2nd D

oo oo oo

ac ac ac

eo eo eo

— How's your slant angle going?

come come come

PRACTICE CONNECTING THESE LETTERS FROM GROUP 4 FEATURING DESCENDING LOOPS.

2nd A
1st A
M
B
1st D
2nd D

ji ji ji

zu zu zu

gl gl gl

— How's your spacing going?

you you you

Joining Letters

Try out these Group 4 letters—featuring ascending loops.

2nd A
1st A
M
B
1st D
2nd D

lb lb lb

hk hk hk

bi bi bi

love love love

- How's your slant angle going?

Group 5 features semi-extended letters.

2nd A
1st A
M
B
1st D
2nd D

te te te

dw dw dw

po po po

time time time

GROUP 6 CONSISTS OF A VARIATION OF DESCENDING LOOPS.

2nd A
1st A
M
B
1st D
2nd D

fa fa fa

fr fr fr

fl fl fl

— A little reminder: check your spacing.

qu qu qu

LETTERS FROM GROUP 8 (R AND S) GO ABOVE THE MEANLINE. HAVE A TRY.

2nd A
1st A
M
B
1st D
2nd D

rt rt rt

sb sb sb

rise rise rise

some some some

Joining Letters

Now have a go at writing words.

2nd A
1st A
M
B
1st D
2nd D

Optimistic Optimistic Optimistic

2nd A
1st A
M
B
1st D
2nd D

Cheerful Cheerful Cheerful

2nd A
1st A
M
B
1st D
2nd D

Excellent Excellent Excellent

2nd A
1st A
M
B
1st D
2nd D

Delightful *Delightful* *Delightful*

2nd A
1st A
M
B
1st D
2nd D

Mercy *Mercy* *Mercy*

2nd A
1st A
M
B
1st D
2nd D

Nice *Nice* *Nice*

Joining Letters

2nd A
1st A
M
B
1st D
2nd D

Humble Humble Humble

2nd A
1st A
M
B
1st D
2nd D

Kind Kind Kind

2nd A
1st A
M
B
1st D
2nd D

Unique Unique Unique

2nd A
1st A
M
B
1st D
2nd D

Vigilant *Vigilant* *Vigilant*

2nd A
1st A
M
B
1st D
2nd D

Warm *Warm* *Warm*

2nd A
1st A
M
B
1st D
2nd D

Xylophone *Xylophone* *Xylophone*

Joining Letters

2nd A
1st A
M
B
1st D
2nd D

Quiet *Quiet* *Quiet*

2nd A
1st A
M
B
1st D
2nd D

Joyful *Joyful* *Joyful*

2nd A
1st A
M
B
1st D
2nd D

Youth *Youth* *Youth*

2nd A
1st A
M
B
1st D
2nd D

Zestful Zestful Zestful

2nd A
1st A
M
B
1st D
2nd D

Truth Truth Truth

2nd A
1st A
M
B
1st D
2nd D

Feel Feel Feel

Joining Letters

2nd A
1st A
M
B
1st D
2nd D

Laugh Laugh Laugh

2nd A
1st A
M
B
1st D
2nd D

Abundant Abundant Abundant

2nd A
1st A
M
B
1st D
2nd D

Inspire Inspire Inspire

2nd A
1st A
M
B
1st D
2nd D

Sweet *Sweet* *Sweet*

2nd A
1st A
M
B
1st D
2nd D

Generous *Generous* *Generous*

2nd A
1st A
M
B
1st D
2nd D

Perfect *Perfect* *Perfect*

Joining Letters

2nd A
1st A
M
B
1st D
2nd D

Refresh Refresh Refresh

2nd A
1st A
M
B
1st D
2nd D

Bliss Bliss Bliss

It´s time to move on to writing phrases.

2nd A
1st A
M
B
1st D
2nd D

Spread kindness

2nd A
1st A
M
B
1st D
2nd D

Cherish the moment

2nd A
1st A
M
B
1st D
2nd D

Live each day to the fullest

Joining Letters

2nd A
1st A
M
B
1st D
2nd D

Be the change you want
to see in the world

Step 6: Flourishing—Elevating Your Handwriting Style

Have some fun with flourishing! But before you dive right in, make sure you have a solid grasp of those basic cursive letterforms.

Flourishes are not only fun, but they are a great way of expressing your unique personality. They can make a certain word stand out, emphasize a point, or create a striking heading. You can go all out with flourishes and be completely over the top. Or just use a few little flourishes to add a pretty touch.

For some people, flourishes come naturally, and they can't wait to show off their style! For others, it can feel totally unnatural, and that's okay too. If that's the case, just keep an open mind and give yourself a chance—you might surprise yourself.

Here are a few more tips on mastering the art of flourishes:

- Remember to keep your arm nice and loose, allowing your flourishes to flow freely—don't hold back!
- Be patient with yourself; flourishing takes practice and time to develop.
- Practice with a pencil first to get a feel for the movement.
- When adding flourishes to your writing, think of it as drawing ovals to achieve smooth and graceful lines. Observe the diagram below—you can spot small ovals within the loops and curves.

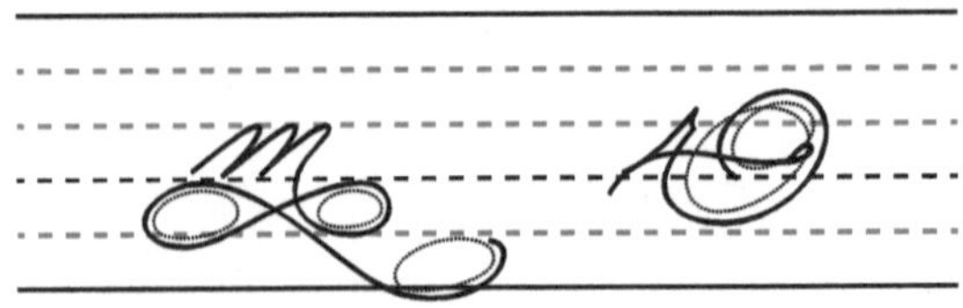

All in all, while flourishes may look fancy, they should still be legible!

Five great places to add flourishes!

1. Ascending Loops

2. Descending Loops

3. The End of Words

4. Underneath Letters

5. In Crossbars

Flourishes

Let's start by practicing some loops and curves, focusing on creating smooth and flowing lines, then flourished letters.

Relax your grip. And if you like, take the pressure off by using a pencil first. Let's go!

2nd A
1st A
M
B
1st D
2nd D

2nd A
1st A
M
B
1st D
2nd D

2nd A
1st A
M
B
1st D
2nd D

2nd A
1st A
M
B
1st D
2nd D
1
2
3
4
5
2nd A
1st A
M
B
1st D
2nd D
1
2
3
4
5
2nd A
1st A
M
B
1st D
2nd D
1
2
3
4
5
6

Flourishes

2nd A
1st A
M
B
1st D
2nd D

3 1 2

2nd A
1st A
M
B
1st D
2nd D

4 1 2 5 3

2nd A
1st A
M
B
1st D
2nd D

4 1 3 5 2

Flourishing Uppercase Letters

When flourishing capitals: don't limit yourself to these examples; it's simply a good starting point. And, as you explore more variations, you may find your own style. It might be simpler, or more complex—anything goes!

If flourishes feel a little intimidating for you, take a look at the example below. You can see that by simply adding one capital letter with a flourish can totally transform the sentence, adding an enchanting touch to your writing!

Don't just exist, live!

First, let's do a little 'flourish warm-up.' Note: you are going to see this particular stem of the capital letter often.

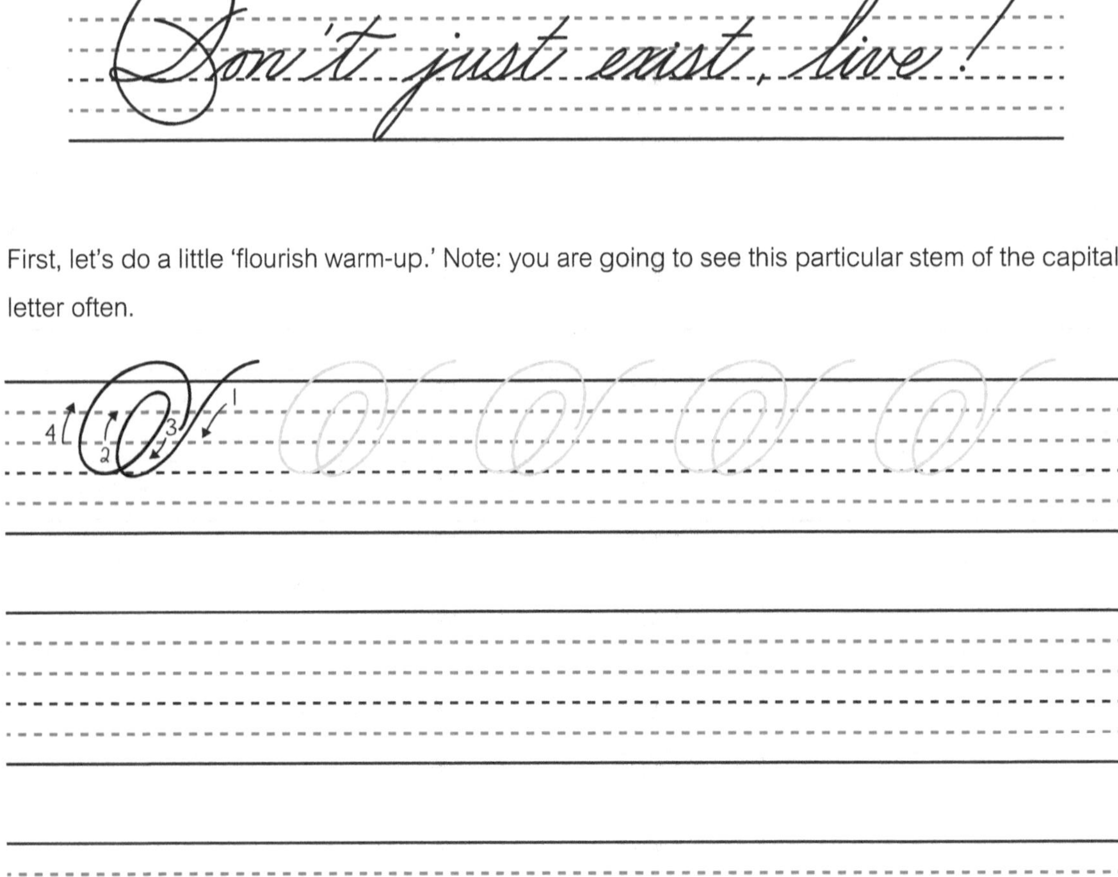

2nd A
1st A
M
B
1st D
2nd D

Flourishes

2nd A
1st A
M
B
1st D
2nd D
1
2
3
4
5
6
7

Flourishes

2nd A
1st A
M
B
1st D
2nd D
1
2
3
4
5
6
7
8

Flourishes

2nd A
1st A
M
B
1st D
2nd D
1
2
3
4
5
6

Flourishes

2nd A
1st A
M
B
1st D
2nd D
1
2
3
4
5
6
7

LET'S TRY ANOTHER SET:

Again, we'll warm up first. Always break down the exercises into manageable steps. If you find yourself struggling with the curves, remember—it's completely normal. Keep going! Like any new skill, as you practice and get the hang of it, you will build up muscle memory and gain better control. It will even become automatic to an extent, like any learned skill. Lastly, don't forget to review the consistency of the slant, shape, and size of your writing.

Just like how we practiced the basic strokes, let's focus on practicing common curve patterns:

2nd A
1st A
M
B
1st D
2nd D
1
2
3
4
5
6
2nd A
1st A
M
B
1st D
2nd D
3
2
1
4
5
6
2nd A
1st A
M
B
1st D
2nd D
1
3
2
5
4
6

Flourishes

2nd A
1st A
M
B
1st D
2nd D
1
2
3
4
5
6
7
2nd A
1st A
M
B
1st D
2nd D
1
2
3
4
5
6
7
2nd A
1st A
M
B
1st D
2nd D
1
2
3
4
5

Flourishes

2nd A
1st A
M
B
1st D
2nd D
1
2
3
4
5
6
7

Flourishes

2nd A
1st A
M
B
1st D
2nd D

Flourishes

2nd A
1st A
M
B
1st D
2nd D
3
1
2
4
5
6
2nd A
1st A
M
B
1st D
2nd D
1
3
2
4
5
6
7

Practice Flourishing Words

One way to practice writing flourishing words is to write the letters in their simplest form first. Remember we discussed the five places where we could add flourishes? Have a go at finding opportunities to enhance the words. Don't give up if it's a bit tricky on the first few tries. It might take some time to get it right.

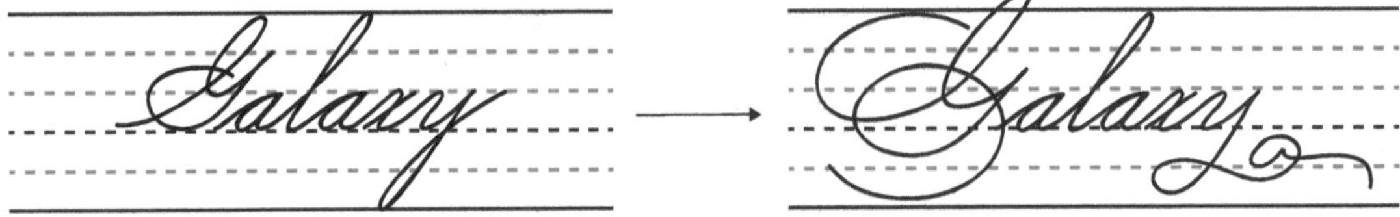

Sometimes flourishes can be quite simple, yet still quite special. They absolutely don't need to be a complex design. You can add that touch of elegance by adding the most subtle of changes by, for example, extending the exit strokes slightly beyond the typical formation, or adding a gentle curve or loop. Experiment and play!

Words with double letters

Be careful with words that contain double letters, because any inconsistency in their formation becomes really noticeable due to their close proximity. Alternatively, you can write them differently by introducing a subtle twist to each of them. This not only adds visual interest to the word but also enhances its overall aesthetic appeal.

Enjoy practicing the word in basic style first. Then, trace the flourished version of the word.

2nd A
1st A
M
B
1st D
2nd D

Appeal

Appeal

2nd A
1st A
M
B
1st D
2nd D

Butterfly

Butterfly

2nd A
1st A
M
B
1st D
2nd D

Challenge

Challenge

Flourishes

2nd A
1st A
M
B
1st D
2nd D

Galaxy

Galaxy

Galaxy

2nd A
1st A
M
B
1st D
2nd D

Helpful

Helpful

Helpful

2nd A
1st A
M
B
1st D
2nd D

Idealistic

Idealistic

Idealistic

Flourishes

2nd A
1st A
M
B
1st D
2nd D

Jellyfish

Jellyfish

Jellyfish

2nd A
1st A
M
B
1st D
2nd D

Kitten

Kitten

Kitten

2nd A
1st A
M
B
1st D
2nd D

Lamp

Lamp

Lamp

2nd A
1st A
M
B
1st D
2nd D

Marvelous Marvelous Marvelous

2nd A
1st A
M
B
1st D
2nd D

Natural Natural Natural

2nd A
1st A
M
B
1st D
2nd D

Orange Orange Orange

Flourishes

2nd A
1st A
M
B
1st D
2nd D

Paper

Paper

Paper

2nd A
1st A
M
B
1st D
2nd D

Quirky

Quirky

Quirky

2nd A
1st A
M
B
1st D
2nd D

Radiant

Radiant

Radiant

2nd A
1st A
M
B
1st D
2nd D

Serene

2nd A
1st A
M
B
1st D
2nd D

Tenacious

2nd A
1st A
M
B
1st D
2nd D

Umbrella

Flourishes

2nd A
1st A
M
B
1st D
2nd D

Vibrant

2nd A
1st A
M
B
1st D
2nd D

Weather

2nd A
1st A
M
B
1st D
2nd D

Xmas

2nd A
1st A
M
B
1st D
2nd D

Young

Young

Young

2nd A
1st A
M
B
1st D
2nd D

Zucchini

Zucchini

Zucchini

Flourishes

Phrases and sentences for you to practice :

2nd A
1st A
M
B
1st D
2nd D

Open your mind

2nd A
1st A
M
B
1st D
2nd D

Don't wait for opportunity.
Create it.

2nd A
1st A
M
B
1st D
2nd D

2nd A
1st A
M
B
1st D
2nd D
Live in the present moment.
The only way to do great
work is to love what you do.

Some words for you to have a go at flourishing!

1. Start by practicing the words in their most basic form if you're feeling a little unsure.
2. Begin with simpler flourishes and gradually work your way up.
3. If it comes naturally, flourish away!

2nd A
1st A
M
B
1st D
2nd D

Tranquil

2nd A
1st A
M
B
1st D
2nd D

Future

2nd A
1st A
M
B
1st D
2nd D

Angelic

2nd A
1st A
M
B
1st D
2nd D

Fulfill

2nd A
1st A
M
B
1st D
2nd D

Genuine

FLOURISHES

2nd A
1st A
M
B
1st D
2nd D

Sincere

2nd A
1st A
M
B
1st D
2nd D

Harmonious

2nd A
1st A
M
B
1st D
2nd D

Whimsical

2nd A
1st A
M
B
1st D
2nd D

Jubilant

How did your flourishing practice go? Do you think you are beginning to find your style? Whether you prefer a simpler or more sophisticated style, it's completely up to you. The main thing is that you stay true to what comes naturally to you. Here's another example:

Tranquil *Fulfill* *Harmonious*

Future *Genuine* *Whimsical*

Angelic *Sincere* *Jubilant*

Step 7: Numbers & Punctuation

Just like letters, numbers and punctuation can create a different look to your written pieces when you change their style. Have some fun with it. You've got the skills now to make these numbers your own.

Examples of different styles:

2nd A
1st A
M
B
1st D
2nd D

0 1 2 3 4 5 6 7 8 9 ! ?

2nd A
1st A
M
B
1st D
2nd D

0 1 2 3 4 5 6 7 8 9 ! ?

2nd A
1st A
M
B
1st D
2nd D

0 1 2 3 4 5 6 7 8 9 ! ?

Numbers & Punctuation

Showcase your style with ampersands:

Extra Step:

Discovering other script styles – Pointed Pen Calligraphy and Brush Lettering

You have now learned many skills in this workbook, and the great thing is that these skills can be applied to various script styles. Why not take your new skills to the next level by exploring brush lettering and pointed-pen calligraphy!

Pointed-pen calligraphy

Pointed-pen calligraphy involves using an oblique or straight pen holder with a pointed tip nib. You dip the nib in the inkwell so often it is also referred to as 'dip pen calligraphy.' Something worth noting: if you have enjoyed practicing cursive with a fountain pen, beware that the ink used with a pointed pen often has a thicker consistency. The thick consistency allows for better control over the ink flow to create the desired thick and thin strokes. Never use calligraphy ink in your fountain pen because it might clog up the pen!

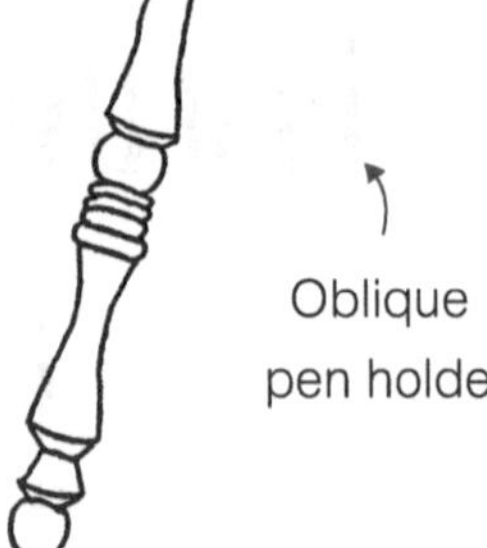

Oblique pen holder

Brush lettering

Brush lettering involves—you guessed it—brushes! Many people opt for brush pens these days which give a fantastic result. This style of writing is characterized by thick downstrokes and thin upstrokes, all created by changing the pressure you place on the pen.

Example of brush lettering alphabet

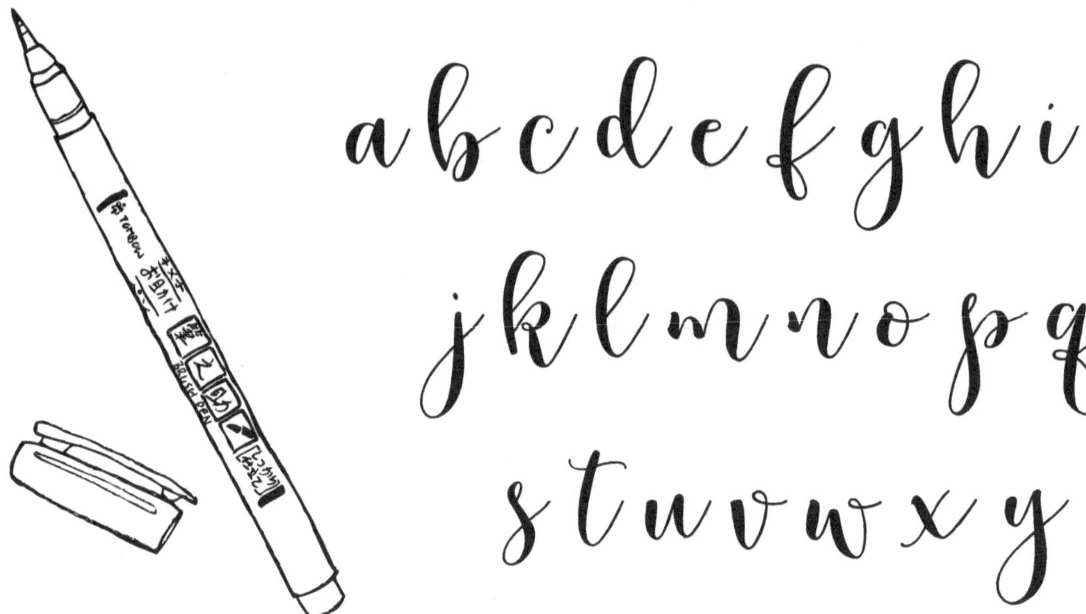

There's so much you can do with brush lettering! Check out calligraphy and lettering artists on websites, in books, or on social media platforms and websites for inspiration. Just like cursive writing, you'll need to be ready to put in some practice and experimentation but, as you already know, practice pays off and the rewards are great!

Check out these comprehensive and easy step-by-step workbooks (in small and large tip) that take you through everything you need to know about brush lettering, and to build upon your new skills. It takes you right through the alphabet, to connecting letters beautifully, adding fancy flourishes, special effects, and more.

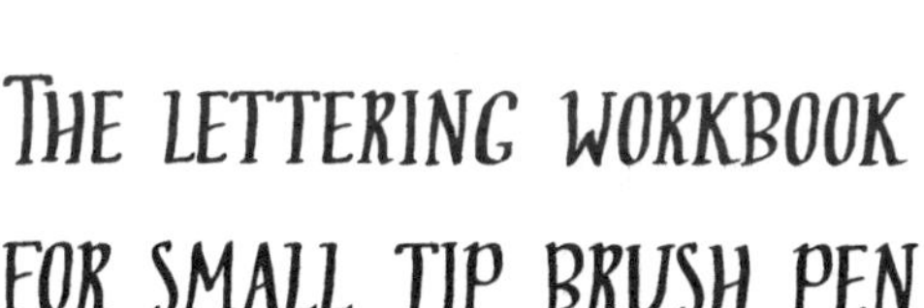

THE LETTERING WORKBOOK
FOR LARGE TIP BRUSH PEN

CONCLUSION

Well done to you for making it to the end of this workbook and for working hard on your cursive writing skills! I hope you found it useful and enjoyable, and that you found your own, unique style too.

Keep working at it and as you continue to refine your skills, we have a special treat for you.

Simply scan the QR code below or enter the following URL https://www.riccagarden.com/cursive-workbook-bonus/. Once you reach the site, kindly share your email address so we can send you the download link for extra practice pages.

HAPPY WRITING!

Made in United States
Troutdale, OR
12/07/2024

26046630R10066